The P...

Pocket
Equine
Dictionary

The Pony Club
Stoneleigh Park
Kenilworth
Warwickshire
CV8 2RW

Website: www.pcuk.org

NOTE TO READERS: If you have any suggestions for equine
terms, words and abbreviations which could be incorporated
into future editions of this dictionary, please write to
The Dictionary Editor at the above address.

© 2011 The Pony Club
Text © 2011 Judith Draper

Concept by Barbara Cooper
Designed and produced by Paul Harding

British Library Cataloguing-in-Publication Data
A catalogue record for this book
is available from the British Library

ISBN 978-1-907279-10-2

Designed and produced by Paul Harding
Printed in Great Britain by Halstan & Co.

Trade distribution by Kenilworth Press
An imprint of Quiller Publishing Ltd
Wykey House, Wykey, Shrewsbury, SY4 1JA
Tel: 01939 261616 Fax: 01939 261606
E-mail: info@quillerbooks.com
Website: www.kenilworthpress.co.uk

The Pony Club
Pocket
Equine
Dictionary

Compiled by Judith Draper

A

Abscess A cavity containing pus (i.e. dead cells, bacteria, etc.).

Action The way in which a horse moves.

Acute In disease, having a short, relatively severe course.

Adrenal In the region of the kidney.

African Horse Sickness A virus infection centred on Africa, though present in other parts of the world, including the Middle East. Spread by mosquitoes and biting midges.

Against the clock In show jumping a competition or jump-off in which, in the case of equality, the competitor with the fastest time wins.

Aged The term used to describe a horse aged seven years and over.

Aids The means by which the rider communicates with the horse. The rider may use the lower legs, the hands, the influence of the body and the seat, and the voice to control the horse. These are known as the natural aids. Whips and spurs are called artificial aids.

Airs above the ground High School movements in which the horse has two or four feet off the ground. *See* Ballotade, Capriole, Courbette, Croupade, Levade.

Alfalfa *See* Lucerne.

Alimentary canal The tube extending the length of the horse's body from the lips to the anus, in which digestion of food occurs.

Angleberry A wart-like growth on the skin.

Animalintex A commercially produced poultice consisting of impregnated cotton-wool protected by gauze which when applied is covered with a thin piece of plastic to retain heat or cold.

Ankle In the USA the term for the fetlock.

Anti-sweat rug A lightweight rug used on a sweating horse while cooling down to prevent chills.

Anti-weaving grille A metal grille fixed to the lower door of a loose-box. The horse can still put his head over the stable door but cannot weave from side to side at the same time. *See also* Weaving.

Artery A tube with a thick wall of elastic tissue and muscle which is part of the system that conveys blood around the body. Arterial blood is bright red due to the high oxygen content.

Arthritis Joint inflammation caused by trauma, infection or stress.

Ascarid *See* Whiteworm.

Ass An equine animal similar to a donkey.

Atherstone girth A leather girth shaped back from the elbows to prevent chafing.

Atlas The first cervical (neck) vertebra articulating with the skull. *See also* Vertebra.

Atrial fibrillation A condition in which the heart beats irregularly (arrhythmia).

Australian cheeker A rubber device which fits over the bit rings on either side of the mouth and runs up the face to a fastening on the headpiece. Designed to keep the bit up in the horse's mouth.

Azoturia A condition causing the horse to become stiff and unwilling to move either during or immediately after exercise. Some muscles, particularly over the hind quarters, become hard and painful; breathing and pulse rates rise, and urine may be red or brown. *Also known as* Setfast or Tying up.

B

Bacteria Extremely small organisms which multiply by simple division. Also called germs, microbes, micro-organisms.

Balance A horse is said to be in balance when his own weight and that of his rider are distributed in such a way as to allow him to use himself with ease and efficiency.

Ballotade A High School air above the ground in which the horse is almost parallel to the ground at the summit of the leap. The forelegs are bent at the knees. The shoes of the hind feet are shown although the legs are not stretched out.

Bar The part of the upper gum of the lower jaw that lies between the horse's incisors (front teeth) and the molars (back teeth). It is on the bars, which have no teeth, that the bit rests.

Barley A cereal grain that may be fed to horses.

Barren A broodmare who is not in foal.

Bar shoe A horse shoe having an additional bar joining both heels and supporting the frog.

Bars of the foot Ridges on the bearing-surface of the foot which are fused with the sole and allow for expansion of the foot.

Bay A coat-colouring of any shade of brown, with black mane and tail and often black points (legs from the knees and hocks downwards).

Bib martingale A combination of a running and an Irish martingale. A leather bib fills the space where the running martingale becomes divided into two straps.

Big knee A swelling on the front of the knee, often caused by a kick, a fall or by hitting a fence.

Big leg Hot, painful swellings beneath the skin of the leg, caused by infection or over-feeding.

Black A coat-colouring where the horse's coat, limbs, mane and tail are black. A black horse may have white markings on the face and legs.

Blacksmith Someone who forges iron. The word blacksmith is often used to describe a farrier, or shoer of horses, because of the close association of the two trades in former times.

Blanket clip A method of clipping a horse whereby the coat is removed from the neck, chest, belly and upper part of the hind legs (and the head, if required). The hair left on the back and rump resembles the shape of a blanket.

Blaze A white marking over the horse's forehead and the bridge of the nose.

Bleeder A horse who suffers from nosebleeds.

Blemish A visible defect, such as a scar, capped hock or spavin, which does not affect a horse's action but which may lessen its value.

Blinkers Eye shields, attached to a head cover, which limit the horse's ability to see behind or to the side. Worn by harness horses and some racehorses.

Blue feet A blue-black hoof colouring seen in some breeds such as Dales and Fell ponies.

Body brush An oval brush with short bristles used for grooming the horse's entire body as well as for brushing the mane and tail.

Bog spavin A swollen hock joint caused by increased synovial fluid, which may be the result of injury, poor conformation or a deficiency in the diet.

Bolting Galloping out of control.

Bolting food Swallowing food without chewing it adequately. May indicate a problem with the horse's teeth, and causes digestive problems.

Bone A measurement of the circumference of the bone immediately beneath a horse's knee or hock.

Bone spavin An arthritic condition of the hock in which a bone or the covering of a bone becomes inflamed.

Booster The common name for the second or subsequent dose of a vaccine.

Boot A protective cover for part of a leg. Used when a horse is travelling or competing, or to keep a dressing in place.

Boot jack A device for removing riding boots.

Bosal A type of bitless bridle.

Bot A fly resembling a bee that is active in early summer and again in September. It lays its eggs on the horse's legs and the horse may then lick and swallow the eggs.

Bounce A distance between two obstacles which is so short that the horse must take off at the second obstacle immediately after landing over the first, without taking a stride.

Bowed tendons Common name for inflamed deep and superficial flexor tendons, and their sheaths, in the forelegs.

Box-walking A habit of walking continuously around the stable. Usually caused by stress or boredom.

Boxy Common name for a foot that is markedly upright. *Also known as* a club foot.

Braids The US term for plaits.

Bran A foodstuff obtained from the outer coat of cereal grain (usually wheat).

Breaking out Profuse sweating that sometimes occurs after a horse has previously dried off. It is usually caused by very hard work or over-excitement.

Breast The front part of the horse's chest, in front of the forelegs.

Breast-girth A web or elastic strap fitted across the horse's breast to prevent the saddle from slipping back. It is attached to the girth-straps on either side of the saddle.

Breast-plate A leather neck-strap attached to the Ds at the front of the saddle and to the girth by a strap passing between the horse's forelegs. It is used to prevent the saddle from slipping back.

Breeching A broad leather band which passes behind a harness horse's hind quarters and takes the weight of a vehicle when going downhill, stopping or backing.

Breed A division within the species *equus caballus.* For example, the Shire Horse and Exmoor Pony.

Bridoon The small snaffle bit used in a double bridle.

Brisket The area of a horse's body over the sternum or breastbone.

Broken-kneed Describes a horse whose knees have been scarred by injury.

Broken wind *See* COPD (chronic obstructive pulmonary disease).

Brood mare A mare used for breeding.

Browband A strap attached to the bridle. It passes to the front of the horse's ears and prevents the headpiece from slipping down the neck.

Brown A coat-colouring which comprises a mixture of black and brown hairs, with black limbs, mane and tail. A very dark brown horse may appear almost black.

Brush The tail of a fox.

Brushing When a horse knocks one foot against the opposite limb.

Buckle-guard A piece of leather attached to the saddle under the flap, or a detachable piece of leather with slots for the girth straps to pass through. Prevents the girth buckles from damaging the saddle-flap.

Bulbs of heel The back part of the horse's foot.

Bulk food *See* Roughage.

Bullfinch A high hedge. The top is thin and may be jumped through rather than over.

Bursa A sac or cavity filled with fluid. Bursas are found where friction occurs: for example in the horse's joints.

Bute *See* phenylbutazone.

C

Camped A conformational defect in which the legs extend too far from the horse's body. 'Camped in front' refers to the forelegs, 'camped behind' to the hind legs.

Canine A pointed tooth which occurs between the incisors and molars in male horses and in some mares.

Canker A vegetative growth of the sensitive frog and sometimes the sole, caused by exposure to ammonia found in wet bedding and uncleaned feet.

Cannon The bone between the knee or hock and the fetlock.

Canter A three-time pace in which the horse's footfalls are as follows: (1) near hind, (2) off hind and near fore together, (3) off fore or (1) off hind, (2) near hind and off fore together, (3) near fore. When the near hind strikes the ground first the horse is said to be cantering on the right leg; when the off hind strikes the ground first the horse is cantering on the left leg. *See also* Collected Canter, Counter Canter, Extended Canter, Medium Canter, Working Canter.

Cantle The back of a saddle.

Capped elbow A swelling at the point of the elbow caused by an inflamed bursa or by bruising. Often the result of the horse striking himself with a hind foot when getting up.

Capriole A High School air above the ground in which the horse jumps up and forward high into the air and then kicks out with both hind legs, landing on all four legs.

Carbohydrate An energy-producing substance that occurs in vegetable and animal tissue. Horses derive carbohydrates from grass and other forage, and also from cereals.

Carcinoma A type of malignant growth (i.e. one that spreads).

Cardiac Relating to the heart (from the Greek *kardiakos* meaning heart).

Caries—Chestnut

Caries The decay or death of bone.

Carotid The main artery in the neck.

Carpal Of the carpus or knee.

Carpitis Inflammation of the knee.

Cartilage The connective tissue which caps the bones that form joints. Cartilage provides a surface for movement.

Cast Unable to stand up from a lying position because of the proximity of a solid structure such as a stable wall or fence.

Cavesson (1) A simple type of noseband. (2) A form of headcollar, with a padded noseband and fitted with swivel rings. Used for lungeing the horse. *See* Lungeing.

Chambon A schooling device used to gradually lower the horse's head, round his back and engage the hind quarters. A strap runs from the girth between the forelegs and divides into two cords which pass through rings attached to a poll-pad. The cords are then fastened to the bit-rings.

Chaps A leather garment which covers the rider's legs but not the seat (from the Spanish *Chaparajos*).

Cheek (of bit) The shank of the bit.

Cheekpiece The part of the bridle to which the bit-ring is attached. The cheekpiece is attached to the headpiece.

Chest The part of the horse's body bounded by the ribcage and diaphragm.

Chestnut (1) A coat colouring that varies from pale gold to liver. (2) A horny growth above the inside of the knee joint and below the inside of the hock. Thought to be the remains of a hoof lost during evolution. Chestnuts are believed to be as individual as a human's fingerprints.

Choke An obstructed gullet. Caused by food or sometimes chewed wood.

Chronic Long-lasting (of disease).

Chukka A period of play in the game of polo.

Cinch American term for the girth on a Western saddle.

Clench (clinch) The part of a horseshoe nail that can be seen on the outside of the hoof-wall. It is flattened by the farrier and rasped smooth.

Clipping The removal of part or all of a horse's coat to enable him to work without sweating excessively. *See also* Blanket Clip, Full Clip, Hunter Clip, Neck and Belly Clip, Trace Clip.

Club foot An abnormality of the foot in which the angle of the hoof-wall from the ground is more than 60 degrees and the heel is high.

Coat The hair which covers the horse's skin.

Coffin The joint between the second and third phalanges (pastern bones below the fetlock joint) and the navicular bone.

Colic Pain that occurs in the abdomen, usually as a result of a disturbance in the alimentary canal.

Collected canter A canter in which the strides are shorter than in working canter. The horse covers less ground and the speed (i.e. miles per hour, not the speed of the rhythm) is decreased. *See also* Rhythm.

Collected trot A trot in which the steps are shorter and higher than in working trot, although the rhythm and tempo are the same.

Collected walk A walk which shows great activity, with each step being higher and shorter than in medium walk.

Colostrum The thick milk produced by a mare at the birth of a foal. Commonly called 'first milk', it is high in protein and gives the foal its immunity against disease.

Colt Young male horse up to the age of four or five.

Combination In show jumping an obstacle comprising three fences but numbered as one fence with elements (a), (b) and (c). The elements may be one or two strides apart.

Conformation The arrangement and proportion of the parts of the horse's body.

Connemara A breed of British native pony originating in Western Ireland.

Contracted heels Heels that are too narrow: something which may be partially corrected by fitting a T or bar shoe to increase pressure on the frog. *See also* Bar shoe.

Corn (1) A term used to describe various dried food given to horses. (2) A bruise of the laminae of the sole of the foot. A corn may be the result of treading on a stone or may be caused by incorrect shoeing or trimming of the foot.

Coronary band The sensitive hoof structure around the upper border of the hoof.

Coronet A white leg marking above the hoof.

Corrective trimming and shoeing Trimming and shoeing the hoof to make it a normal shape and correctly balanced.

Counter canter A movement in which the horse canters to the left with the right leg leading, and vice versa.

Courbette A High School air above the ground in which the horse assumes the position of almost a full rear and then jumps forward from his hocks a number of times, landing each time with the hocks bent and the position of the rear maintained.

Cow hocks Hocks which, seen from behind, are too close together, with the feet splayed out.

Cracked heels *See* Mud fever.

Cream A coat colouring. *Also known as* cremello.

Croup The part of the hind quarters from the highest point to the top of the tail.

Croupade A High School air above the ground in which the horse kicks high in the air with both hind feet, keeping the front feet on the ground.

Curb An enlargement at the back of the hind leg at the top end of the cannon bone about 15 cm (6in) below the point of the hock. Often caused by a sprain or trauma.

Curry comb (1) A metal tool used for cleaning the body brush during grooming.
(2) A rubber or plastic implement used for removing caked mud from a grass-kept horse or pony.

Cushing's disease A condition in which the horse grows an excessively shaggy coat, is very thirsty and is prone to laminitis. It is caused by an overgrowth of a type of cell in the pituitary gland, which is connected to the base of the brain.

D

D (or Dee) A metal fitting on a saddle, shaped like a letter D, to which an item such as a breastplate may be attached.

Dales A breed of British native pony originally bred on the east side of the Pennine Hills in northern England.

Dam The female parent of a horse or pony.

Dandy brush A brush with strong bristles used for removing dried mud from a horse's coat.

Dartmoor A breed of British native pony originating on Dartmoor.

Deep litter A method of bedding in which the droppings are regularly removed but the wet bedding remains and is covered with fresh bedding. The entire bedding is removed periodically.

Diagonal When the horse trots, his feet strike the ground in diagonal pairs (near fore together with off hind, off fore together with near hind). In rising trot the rider is said to be riding on the left diagonal if the seat returns to the saddle as the near fore and off hind touch the ground; the rider is on the right diagonal if the seat returns to the saddle as the off fore and near hind touch the ground.

Digital cushion The fatty pad at the back of the horse's foot, above the frog. It forms the bulbs of the heel and reduces concussion when the foot hits the ground.

Direct rein A leading or opening rein. The action of this rein turns the horse's head towards the direction in which it is required to move.

Dish face A face with a concave profile, typical of Arab horses.

Dishing Faulty action in which the foot of one or both forelegs is thrown outwards below the knee.

Disunited A term which describes the canter when the horse's leading hind leg is on the opposite side to his leading foreleg.

Dock The flesh and bone part of the horse's tail.

Dr Bristol A type of bit with an oval plate in the centre of the snaffle mouthpiece.

Dr Green A term used to describe the benefits of turning a lame horse away to grass for rest.

Double Two show jumping obstacles placed within one or two strides of each other and judged as one fence, parts (a) and (b).

Double bridle Bridle with two bits, a snaffle (known as a bridoon) and a curb (Weymouth), and two reins.

Drag hunting Hunting with a pack of hounds who follow an artificial scent, or drag, laid by a person trailing a suitably scented item.

Drawing-knife A knife with a narrow blade and the point bent over for safety. Used by a farrier to trim the hoof-wall and the frog.

Draw-rein A severe means of control comprising a rein which is attached to the girth and passes through the bit-rings to the rider's hands.

Dressage A word deriving from the French *dresser* (to train or adjust), used since the 18th Century to describe the systematic training of horses and now used to describe the competitive discipline.

Drop (fence) An obstacle where the landing side is lower than the take-off.

Drop noseband A noseband which is fastened below the bit.

Droppings The solid waste eliminated by a horse. *Also known as 'dung'.*

Dun A coat-colouring which can vary from yellow (a light, sandy coloured coat) to blue. Dun horses have black skin, mane and tail and may have a dorsal or 'eel' stripe. Some dun horses have stripes on their withers and legs. These are known as zebra markings and may be the remains of a form of camouflage.

Eel stripe A continuous dark-coloured stripe extending from the line of the neck to the tail.

Eggbutt A type of snaffle bit designed to prevent the mouthpiece from sliding through the mouth and to minimise the chances of the bit pinching the lips.

Elbow The upper foreleg joint.

Electrolytes Essential chemicals present in solution in the blood. *Also known as* blood salts. They include sodium and potassium. If there is excessive loss of these salts through sweating when the horse is in hard work, particularly in hot weather, they may be replaced by adding them to the horse's drinking water.

Elk lip A wide, overhanging upper lip.

Entire Another term for a stallion.

Eohippus A small animal which lived in the Eocene period about 55 million years ago. Eohippus is the ancestor of today's horse.

Equestrian (1) Pertaining to horses and horsemanship. (2) A person who rides on horseback.

Equidae Members of the horse family, including horses, asses, zebras and onagers.

Equine Of the horse family (*Equidae*).

Equus Genus of the horse family.

Equus Caballus All breeds of domesticated horse and their feral or wild relatives

Ergot A small, horny area

situated in the tuft of hair behind the fetlock joint.

Ermine marks Small black or brown marks on a white background. They are found around the coronet and resemble ermine fur.

Ewe neck A neck where the crest (between the poll and the withers) is concave rather than convex. *Also known as an upside-down neck.*

Extended canter A canter in which the horse covers as much ground as possible without losing calmness or changing the rhythm and tempo.

Extended trot A trot in which the horse covers as much ground as possible with every step, increasing the speed while maintaining the same rhythm and tempo as in medium trot.

Extended walk A walk in which the horse covers as much ground as possible, increasing the speed without losing the regularity of the steps, and maintaining the same rhythm and tempo as in medium walk.

Extension The lengthening of a horse's stride within the pace and without loss of balance or rhythm.

Extensor Any muscle or tendon which extends a joint.

F

Farrier A craftsman who shoes horses.

Feather The common name for the long hair found on the lower legs of some horses and ponies.

Feather-edged shoe
A shoe designed to prevent brushing. *See also* Brushing.

Fell A breed of British native pony originating from the western side of the Pennine Hills in northern England.

Femur The large bone situated between the hip joint and the stifle joint.

Feral A free-roaming animal, descended from escaped captive animals. Feral breeds of horses include the Brumby in Australia and the Mustang in North America.

Fetlock The foreleg or hind leg joint formed by the cannon, pastern and sesamoid bones.

Fibula A small, slender bone attached at the upper and lower ends to the tibia, which is situated between the stifle joint and the hock.

Fillet string A cord attached to the rear corners of some rugs and exercise sheets. It passes under the tail and helps to keep the clothing in place on windy days.

Filly Female horse up to the age of four or five.

Fistulous withers An abscess, usually the result of a wound which has become infected with bacteria.

Fixed cheek A curb bit in which there is no movement between the mouthpiece and the cheek.

Flash noseband A caves-son noseband to which an extra strap is fitted which fastens below the bit. May be used when a drop noseband

and standing martingale are required.

Flat foot A foot in which the sole lacks the normal concave surface.

Flehmen posture An extended neck and head, with the upper lip curled back. Seen in mares in the early stages of labour; in stallions, and sometimes when a horse is suffering from colic.

Flexor A muscle or tendon which flexes a joint.

Floating Rasping down the sharp edges which form on a horse's molar teeth.

Flute bit A bit with a perforated, hollow mouthpiece. Used to prevent horses from wind-sucking, it works by dispersing the gulp of air. *See also*

Wind-sucking.

Fly cap A net worn over the ears to protect against flies.

Fly fringe A fringe attached to a browband. Designed to keep flies away from the horse's eyes.

Flying change A change of leading leg at the canter.

Foal A colt, filly or gelding up to the age of 12 months.

Forage Foodstuffs, specifically bulk food such as grass or hay.

Forearm The part of the front legs extending from the elbow to the knee.

Forging When the toe of a hind foot strikes the bottom of the front foot of the same side.

Founder *See* Laminitis

Fracture A break in a bone. There are several different types of fracture, including hairline (very small), greenstick (the bending of young bone), impacted (one end of a bone driven into another), compound (where the bone is exposed by a skin wound) and comminuted (many pieces).

Freeze branding A system of permanent marking for identification purposes. The pigment cells of the hair are killed with intense cold.

French link A snaffle bit with a connecting link in the centre.

Frog The wedge-shaped mass found on the underside of the hoof between the bars and the sole. It contains about 50 per cent water and is part of the weight-bearing structure of the foot.

Full brothers, full sisters Horses having the same sire and dam.

Full clip A method of clipping a horse whereby the entire coat is removed, including from the legs.

Fulmer snaffle A loose-ring jointed snaffle fitted with cheekpieces.

Furlong A distance, used in racing, of one-eighth of a mile (220 yards or 200 metres).

Furniture The metal mountings on saddlery and harness.

G

Gag (1) A bit with holes in the rings through which a rounded rope/leather cheekpiece is passed. (2) A device for holding the horse's mouth open during, for example, dental treatment.

Gait The sequence of leg movements of a horse.

Gallop A four-beat pace or gait: a faster version of the canter.

Gallops Specially prepared and maintained areas of land used by trainers to prepare horses for racing.

Galvayne's groove A groove which runs down the length of the corner incisor teeth. Found in most horses and a rough indicator of age. Named after the 19th-century Australian-born horse trainer Sydney Galvayne.

Gamgee A type of padding, comprising absorbent cotton wool covered with absorbent gauze, used under leg bandages. Named after its inventor, Joseph Gamgee (1826-1886), a qualified doctor and veterinary surgeon.

Gaskin The part of the hind leg between the stifle and the hock. *Also known as* the second thigh.

Goose rump Hind quarters that slope sharply from the croup to the dock.

Grakle A type of noseband with two straps, one fastening above the bit, the other below. Named after the 1931 Grand National winner, who wore one.

Grass sickness A serious condition of the alimentary canal (*see* Gut) which is often fatal. Symptoms include constipation, depression, a fast pulse and sweating.

Greasy heel *See* Mud fever.

Ground line The line at the base of an obstacle, used by the horse to assess his take-off. A clearly defined ground line, such as a pole on the ground, is known as a true ground line and makes it easier for the horse to judge the fence. A false ground line is one where the base of an obstacle is pushed back beyond the line of the vertical face of the fence. A false ground line confuses the horse

Gut Another name for the intestine, bowel or alimentary canal.

Gymnastic jumping A method of training the horse to jump and to improve his jumping skills by using a series of small obstacles in close succession.

H

Habit The costume worn by a woman or girl riding side-saddle.

Hack (1) To go for a pleasure ride. (2) A type of horse used for pleasure riding.

Hackamore A type of bitless bridle. The horse is controlled by means of pressure on the nose, poll and chin groove.

Hackney A breed of harness horse or pony with a characteristic high-stepping trot.

Haematoma A collection of blood-stained fluid in a muscle, usually caused by a kick or other injury. *Also known as* a blood blister.

Haemorrhage An escape of blood normally contained in the blood vessels (i.e. veins, arteries and capillaries). A haemorrhage occurs when a blood vessel breaks, and may be internal or external.

Half-bred Having one Thoroughbred parent.

Half-brothers, half-sisters Horses with the same dam but different sires.

Half-halt A momentary collection of the horse while he is in motion. It is used to increase the horse's attention and balance during a change of direction, speed or pace.

Half-pass A movement in which the horse moves forwards and sideways at the same time. He moves on two tracks, with his shoulders slightly in advance of his hind quarters. His outside legs cross in front of his inside legs.

Half-pirouette *See* Pirouette.

Halter A webbing or rope alternative to a headcollar.

Halter classes In the USA, classes for animals shown in hand.

Hand The term traditionally used to measure a horse's height. One hand equals four inches (the approximate measurement of a human hand).

Handicap (1) A race in which the weights carried by the horses are adjusted by the official handicapper to give each horse, theoretically, an equal chance of winning. (2) In polo, players are given handicaps according to their ability, the best receiving the highest handicaps. The handicaps of each member of a team are added together. The lower team handicap is then subtracted from the higher one to give the number of goals 'start' awarded to the team with the lower handicap.

Handiness The ability of a horse to turn quickly and willingly.

Harness A term used to describe the bridle, collar, pad, traces and other equipment worn by a driven horse.

Hay Grass that has been cut when it is coming into flower and before it has gone to seed and is then dried in the field. Used as a bulk food for stabled horses and a supplementary food for others. Hay produced from permanent pasture, which is not ploughed and re-seeded, is known as Meadow Hay. Hay cut from specially sown fields containing one particular grass, or a variety of grasses, suitable for horses, is known as Seed Hay.

Haylage Cut grass vacuum-packed in small, sealed plastic bags.

Hay-net A strong, corded net used for feeding hay.

Head carriage The natural position of the horse's head and neck.

Headcollar An item of tack with a noseband (which may be adjustable), cheekpieces, throat-lash and adjustable headpiece. Used for leading and tying up. May be made of leather or a synthetic material.

Headcollar rope A strong rope which can be clipped to the metal ring on the underside of a headcollar noseband and used to lead a horse or to tie him up.

Headpiece The part of the bridle which rests behind the horse's ears. The headpiece is a broad band of leather which divides on either side of the horse's head to form the throatlash. In conjunction with the cheekpieces, to which it is attached, the headpiece supports the bit in the horse's mouth.

Headshaking When a horse continuously shakes his head up and down. It is a problem that usually occurs only during exercise and is often worse during the summer. The possible causes range from dental problems to neuralgia.

Head shy A term used to describe a horse reluctant to have his head handled or his headcollar or bridle put on.

Heavy horse A large type or breed of draught horse.

Heel The hindmost part of the foot. *See also* Contracted heels.

Henny The offspring of a jenny (female) donkey and male horse.

Highland A breed of British native pony originating in Scotland.

Hobday An operation to relieve an abnormal breathing noise caused by paralysis of the muscles which control the cartilage in a horse's larynx or voice box. The operation is named after the veterinary surgeon Sir Frederick Hobday.

Hock The joint in the hind leg between the gaskin (second thigh) and the cannon bone. It is the equivalent of the human ankle. *See also* Capped hock.

Hock boots Protective boots, fitted with a top and lower strap, designed to protect the hocks while travelling.

Hogging The complete removal of the mane with clippers.

Hoof The horny casing of the foot.

Hoof oil An oil, specially designed for use on horses, which is painted on the hooves to improve their appearance. Used on special occasions, such as at shows.

Hoof pick An implement used to remove dirt, stones, etc. from a horse's feet.

Horn The hard cells which form the hoof.

Horse-walker A mechanical device for exercising several horses at a time without the need for a rider or leader. A horse-walker is a circular pen divided into sections with partitions fitted on rotating arms. The horses walk around in a circle.

Hosing Applying cold water from a hosepipe to a horse's leg or foot. Used to clean a wound and to reduce swelling and inflammation.

Hot-blooded A term used to describe a high-spirited horse.

Hot up, to When a horse becomes over-excited, especially when ridden.

Humerus The long bone between the shoulder joint and the elbow joint.

Hunter A type of horse suitable for withstanding a day's hunting.

Hunter clip A method of clipping a horse whereby all the coat is removed except for the legs and a patch under the saddle.

I

Impulsion Energy asked for by the rider and supplied by the horse. The horse goes forward actively but does not increase his speed.

Incisor A front tooth. The horse has six incisors in the upper jaw and six in the lower jaw.

Infection A condition caused by bacteria, fungus or a virus.

Inflammation Tissue reaction to injury. Symptoms are heat, swelling, redness and pain.

Influenza A highly infectious disease. Symptoms are cough, watery nasal discharge, loss of appetite, shivering and inflamed throat.

In hand When a horse is led by a person on the ground, without a rider.

Irish martingale A leather strap approximately 4 ins (10 cm) long, with a metal ring attached to each end through which the reins are passed under the horse's neck. Designed to prevent the reins from going over a horse's head. *Also known as* rings.

Isolation When a sick horse is kept in a stable well away from other horses to prevent the possible spread of disease.

J

Jenny A female donkey.

Jockeys Small black deposits of grease and dirt on a saddle flap.

Joint oil *See* Synovial fluid.

Jumper's bump A term used to describe the protuberance at the top of the croup. It was once thought that a pronounced bump increased a horse's ability to jump.

Jumping-lane A long, narrow, fenced-in enclosure used for teaching a horse to jump.

Jump-off The final round in a show-jumping competition. If the riders' scores are still equal, the one with the fastest time is usually the winner.

K

Kaolin A fine clay used in poulticing. *Also known as* china clay.

Keeper A fixed leather loop for retaining a strap on a bridle.

Keratoma A horny tumour in the inner surfaces of the wall of the foot.

Kimblewick A single-rein Pelham bit with a straight bar and small tongue-groove.

Kineton noseband A noseband comprising a leather front-strap attached to a metal loop on each side. The loops are fitted around the mouthpiece of the bit so that pressure on the reins is partially or wholly transferred to the nose.

Knee-caps Protective

covers for the knees, held in place by straps above and below the knee. *Also known as* knee-boots.

Knuckling (1) A condition of young horses in which the forelegs are straight and the fetlock joints permanently flexed. (2) Action when a horse stumbles, which may result from the fetlock joints being too straight.

Kür In competitive dressage, a freestyle test performed to music (from the German meaning 'free exercise').

L

Laburnum An ornamental tree, all parts of which are poisonous.

Lameness A disturbance in the horse's natural gait.

Laminitis An inflamed sensitive lamina of the hoof resulting in heat and pain. *See also* Sensitive lamina.

Lampas A swelling and hardening of the mucous membrane that lines the hard palate of the mouth immediately behind the upper incisors.

Larva The young or immature stage in the life of an insect or parasite such as the redworm.

Larynx A short tube connecting the throat and the windpipe. It regulates the intake of air and protects against the breathing-in of dust. It is the site of the horse's voice. *Also known as* the Voice Box.

Lateral work When the

horse moves forwards and sideways at the same time, with the fore- and hind legs moving on different tracks. *See also* Half-pass.

Laurel An evergreen shrub, poisonous to horses.

Lead-rope A strong rope used for leading and tying up.

Leg-up A method of mounting without using the stirrup or a mounting block. The rider bends his left leg backwards from the knee. An assistant places his left hand under the rider's knee and his right hand under the ankle. At a given signal, the rider jumps upwards from his right foot while the assistant pushes him upwards until he is high enough to be able to

swing his leg over the horse's back.

Leg-yielding A movement used by some trainers when introducing a young horse to lateral work. The horse moves on two tracks. His body is straight except for a slight flexion at the poll away from the direction in which he is going.

Levade A High School air above the ground in which the horse lifts both forefeet off the ground and draws them in whilst the hind quarters, deeply bent in the haunches, bear the entire weight of the body.

Lice Skin parasites with small, flat, wingless bodies.

Ligament The band of fibrous tissue that connects bones or supports organs.

Lip-strap A narrow strap

designed to hold the curb-chain if it becomes unhooked, and to prevent a horse catching hold of the cheeks of the bit with his teeth. It is fastened to the 'D' rings on the bit cheeks.

Lockjaw *See* Tetanus.

Long-reining The driving of a young horse by a trainer on foot. Two separate reins, about 25 ft (7.6 m) long, are used. Long-reining is used to teach the horse various movements without having to carry the weight of a rider.

Loosebox A stable.

Lucerne A nutritious clover-type plant grown and processed in the same way as hay.

Lumbar Of the back.

Lungeing Exercising a horse on a lungeing-rein. The horse moves in a circle around the handler, who controls him by means of the voice, the lungeing rein and the lungeing whip. The horse wears a specially designed lungeing cavesson, to which the rein is attached. Lungeing is a useful way of exercising a horse who cannot be ridden, perhaps because of a sore back, or in order to settle an excitable horse down before mounted work.

Lungworm A slender roundworm that lives in the air passages of the lungs where it lays its eggs, which are coughed up and then swallowed. The swallowed eggs pass out in the droppings, hatch and are picked up by a new host. The larvae bore through the intestinal wall and enter the lymph stream. Blood carries them through the heart and into the lungs, where they develop into adult worms, completing the life cycle. They cause coughing, bronchitis and pneumonia. Donkeys can carry large numbers of lung-worms without showing symptoms.

Lymphangitis
Inflammation of the lymphatic vessels and nodes, usually in the hind limbs. Symptoms are hot, painful swellings and stiffness. Caused by an infection or by the overloading of the lymph stream due to excess feed. *Also known as* 'Monday morning leg'. *See* Lymphatic system.

Lymphatic system
A system of channels similar to veins but without valves. They contain fluid consisting of water, protein, fat and a small number of cells. They are an essential part of the body's fluid balance and defence mechanism. Lymph glands or nodes occur at intervals in the channels and act as filters. The glands prevent microbes spreading through the body.

M

Made A horse is said to be 'made' when his training is complete.

Magenis snaffle A jointed snaffle fitted with revolving rollers set into slits in the mouth pieces.

Maize A high-energy grain.

Manège An outdoor enclosure used for

schooling horses and teaching equitation.

Mane-pulling Removing hair from the mane in order to thin and/or shorten it.

Mange An infective skin condition caused by mites.

Mare A female horse aged from 4 to 5 years up.

Mark The dark centre of the tooth of a young horse.

Market Harborough A type of martingale. At the centre of the chest, where the girth strap and neck strap meet, there is a ring. Attached to the ring are two strips of leather which pass up through the bit-rings and fasten on to the reins. When the horse is carrying his head correctly the strips of leather are slack. They only tighten if he throws his head up.

Markings White markings on the head and legs. *See also* Blaze, Snip, Sock, Star, Stocking, Stripe, White face.

Martingale A device to prevent a horse from carrying his head too high. *See also* Bib martingale, Irish martingale, Market Harborough, Running martingale, Standing martingale,

Martingale stop A leather or rubber stop fitted to each rein to prevent the rings of a running martingale sliding forward and becoming caught on the rein-fastening or on a tooth.

Measuring stick A wooden stick with a sliding right-angle arm, used for measuring the height of a horse. The arm is placed over the horse's withers. The height may be measured in inches, hands and/or centimetres.

Medium canter A pace between working canter and extended canter. The horse covers more ground than in working canter and the strides are rounder and longer. The speed increases but the rhythm and tempo are unchanged.

Medium trot A pace between working and extended trot. The rhythm and tempo remain the same but the horse covers more ground than in working trot. The steps are longer and therefore the speed is increased.

Medium walk A pace between collected and extended walk in which the horse takes even and regular steps and which looks and feels calm, active and purposeful.

Metacarpus The part of the leg between the knee (carpus) and the pastern (phalanx): i.e. the cannon bone.

Metatarsus The area between the hock and the fetlock joint in the hind leg.

Mews Stabling grouped round an open yard or alley (from the French *muer*, a place where moulting falcons were kept).

Microbe A minute living organism, especially one that causes disease.

Molars Large grinding teeth situated beyond the bars of the mouth. The adult horse has 24 permanent molars, six on each side of the upper jaw, six on each side of the lower jaw.

Monday morning disease
See Azoturia.

Monday morning leg
See Lymphangitis.

Moon blindness
Inflammation of the eye. Symptoms include spasm of the eyelids when exposed to light; inflammation of the surface of the eye; tears running down the face, and constriction of the pupils. Possibly caused by infection.

Mouthing bit A bit with 'keys' attached. It is used to encourage a wet mouth.

Mouthpiece That part of a bit which is in the horse's mouth.

Mud fever An infection which enters the skin when horses are exposed to prolonged rain or are in poor condition. It affects the back, belly and lower limbs. The hair becomes matted, scabs form and hair loss occurs. *Also known as* Rainscald or Greasy heel.

Mule The offspring of a male ass and a female horse.

Mullen mouth A bit with a half-moon shaped mouthpiece.

N

Nail-bind Inflammation and pain caused by a nail pressing on the sensitive laminae of the foot.

Nails Specially designed nails used for fixing a shoe to the horses's foot.

Nappy A term used to describe a horse which, through stubbornness or bad temper, refuses to respond to the aids when correctly given.

Nations' Cup An international team show-jumping competition consisting of two rounds over the same course. Each team comprises a minimum of three and maximum of four horse/rider combinations. A team's three lowest scores from each round are added together to give their total score.

Native pony A breed of pony native to the British Isles. The nine British native pony breeds are: Connemara, Dales, Dartmoor, Exmoor, Fell, Highland, New Forest, Shetland and Welsh. They are *Also known as* Mountain and Moorland ponies.

Navicular bone A boat-shaped bone situated in the foot behind the coffin bone.

Navicular syndrome Inflammation of the bursa, deep flexor tendon and navicular bone, causing pain and lameness.

Near side The left-hand side of the horse.

Neatsfoot oil A type of oil used to keep leather supple.

Neck and belly clip A method of clipping a horse whereby the coat is removed from under the neck and along the underside of the belly. Variations to this type of clip are the Bib clip, in which only the coat from the underside of the neck down in front of the chest is removed, and the Apron clip, in which the coat is removed down to the girth line between the front legs and from the top of the forelegs.

Neckstrap A narrow leather strap that fits around the horse's neck. Used in an emergency when the rider needs something to hold on to: for example when learning to jump or riding a young horse.

Neigh A horse's loud call that may express anxiety, pleasure or surprise.

Nettle rash Multiple small, inflamed, raised weals on the skin, caused by an allergic reaction to plant pollens. *Also known as* Urticaria.

New Forest A breed of British native pony originating in the New Forest in southern England.

Nicker A horse's soft call denoting pleasurable anticipation.

Nits *See* Lice.

Nosebag A type of portable manger which is hung on the horse's head.

Noseband The part of the bridle which fastens around the horse's nose. The noseband is held in place by a narrow strap passing behind the horse's ears. *See also* Cavesson, Drop noseband, Flash noseband, Grakle noseband, Kineton noseband.

Numnah A saddle-shaped pad fitted under the saddle to protect the horse's back.

Nuts A manufactured foodstuff containing a mixture of ingredients, including vitamins and minerals. *Also known as* cubes.

O

Oak poisoning Caused by a horse eating the leaves or acorns of the oak tree. Symptoms include loss of appetite and constipation, which are sometimes followed by diarrhoea, excessive urination and a watery discharge from the eyes.

Oats A high-energy grain food which may be fed whole, bruised, rolled or crushed.

Oedema An abnormal accumulation of fluid outside cells. It collects in spaces below the skin, resulting in soft swellings. Causes include infection, malnutrition, heart disease, kidney disease, too much food, and inflammation.

Off side The right-hand side of the horse.

One-day event A competition consisting of dressage, show jumping and cross-country, usually run in that order on the same day.

On the leg An expression indicating that a horse has over-long legs for his size.

Opthalmia Inflammation of the eye.

Outline The line of the horse's body when in motion.

Over at the knee A forward curve of the knees when viewed from the side.

Overbent A defective position of the head when the horse is in motion. The head approaches the chest to a point beyond the vertical.

Over-faced A horse

43

who is asked to jump beyond his ability.

Over-horsed A rider whose horse is too large or too strong for him.

Over-reach boots Bell-shaped protective boots which fit around the pastern and encompass the hoof.

Over-reaching Action in which the hind foot steps on the heel of the forefoot on the same side.

Over-shot mouth *See* Parrot mouth.

Over-tracking When the horse's hind foot passes over the print left by the forefoot on the same side.

P

Paddock An enclosed area of grassland.

Pad saddle A type of saddle made of felt which may be partially or wholly covered with leather and which has either no tree or only a tree forepart. Pad-saddles are designed for small children.

Palate A partition separating the mouth from the nasal cavities.

Pan American Games Events based on the Olympic Games but limited to nations in North, South and Central America. They are held every four years in the year preceding the Olympics and include dressage, eventing and show jumping.

Panel The cushioned part of a saddle between the tree and the horse's back.

Paper bedding A dust-free

bedding material consisting of shredded paper.

Parasite A creature which lives on or in another animal. External equine parasites include mites and lice. Internal parasites include various types of worm and maggot.

Parrot mouth A malformation of the upper jaw, where the front teeth overhang the lower jaw. *Also known as* an over-shot mouth.

Passage A very cadenced lofty trot with a marked moment of suspension.

Pastern The part of the leg between the fetlock and coronet.

Peacock stirrup-iron A safety iron in which a strong ring of rubber replaces the metal on the outside, making it less likely for the foot to become trapped in the event of a fall.

Pedal bone A bone inside the horse's foot. *Also known as* the coffin bone or third phalanx.

Pedalostitis Inflammation of the pedal bone, causing pain and lameness.

Pelham A bit combining the action of a bridoon and curb in one mouthpiece. The bridoon and curb reins are attached to separate rings.

Pelham roundings Curved leather couplings joining the bridoon and curb rings of a Pelham bit so that one rein can be used instead of two.

Penicillin A powerful antibiotic.

Phalanx One of three bones below the fetlock joint.

Phenylbutazone A fine,

creamy-white odourless powder used to treat painful conditions. *Also known as* Bute.

Piaffe A passage performed on the spot, with minimal forward movement.

Piebald A coat-colouring featuring irregular patches of black and white hair.

Pigeon toes Toes which turn inwards. *Also known as* pin toes.

Pinworm Worms that live just inside the rectum and lay their eggs around the anus, causing irritation. *Also known as Oxyuris equi.*

Pirouette A movement in which the horse completes a turn of 360°, with the forehand making a circle around the inside hind leg. A turn through 180° is a half-pirouette.

Placing pole A pole set on the ground on the take-off side of a fence to help a horse to arrive at the right place for take-off.

Plaiting (1) Faulty action in which as the horse puts his feet to the ground he swings them inwards. (2) Putting the mane and the top hairs of the tail into plaits. *See also* Braiding.

Pneumonia Inflamed lung tissue.

Poached A term used to describe muddy, badly cut-up ground, for example in a gateway or on the take-off side of a fence.

Pointing Standing with the toe of a foreleg pointing.

Poll The highest point of the horse's head just behind the ears.

Poll-evil An infection of the poll area with painful swellings on one or both sides of the neck.

Poll-guard A felt and leather pad which fits on to the headcollar to protect the top of the horse's head when travelling.

Pommel (1) The raised, arched part of the front of an astride saddle. (2) Either of the two projecting parts on the near-side of a side-saddle.

Pony A member of the *equus caballus* family standing no more than 14.2 hh.

Port The arched section of the mouthpiece of a curb bit which provides room for the horse's tongue.

Poulticing The application of a hot or cold substance to draw dirt, maggots or pus from an affected area.

Prophet's thumb mark A dimple sometimes found on the neck of horses, particularly Arabs. Believed to be a sign of great luck.

Propping The slowing-down action of a horse who is reluctant to take off at a fence.

Pulmonary Of the lungs.

Pupil The opening at the centre of the iris of the eye.

Purebred A horse whose blood is not mixed with that of other breeds or types.

Pus Inflammatory product consisting of bacteria, cells and fluid. *See also* Abscess.

Q

Quadrille A display to music by a group of horses and riders.

Quagga A type of Burchell's zebra hunted to extinction in the 19th century.

Quarantine A period in which a horse is isolated to prevent the spread of an infectious disease.

Quartering A quick grooming to make a horse look tidy before exercise.

Quarter marks Decorative patterns brushed into the hair on the horse's hind quarters.

Quarter sheet A sheet placed under the saddle during exercise or over the saddle of a racehorse when parading in the paddock.

Quidding Dropping quantities of chewed grass or hay from the mouth.

Quittor Necrosis of the lateral cartilage of the foot due to infection, with severe lameness and pus.

R

Rack A fast pace in which each foot strikes the ground singly.

Rack-chain A chain attached to a headcollar and used to tie a horse up.

Radius The larger of the two bones of the forearm, between the elbow joint and the knee.

Ragwort A poisonous plant which causes

progressive damage to the liver and may prove fatal. Symptoms include weakness, a rapid pulse and breathing, constipation, jaundice, yawning and staggering.

Random Three horses driven in single file.

Rangy A term describing a horse with plenty of size and scope.

Rasping The removal of sharp edges on the teeth with a rasp. *Also known as* floating, especially in the USA.

Red ribbon A piece of ribbon worn around the top of the tail of a horse who kicks as a warning to other riders.

Redworm Small worms which thrive in the horse's intestine and suck blood.

Refuse To stop in front of an obstacle and refuse to jump it.

Rein-back A backward movement of the horse in which the left hind and right forelegs are moved together and the right hind and left fore.

Renal Of the kidney.

Rhinitis Inflamed mucous membranes of the nose.

Rhythm The regularity and evenness of the horse's hoof beats.

Ribbons Coloured rosettes awarded at shows.

Ringbone A growth of new bone on the first, second or third phalanx due to inflamed bone lining. Caused by trauma, underlying bone disease, nutritional deficiency or infection.

Rings *See* Irish martingale.

Ringworm A condition caused by fungal invasion of skin cells and

N O P Q R S T U V W X Y Z

hair fibres. No type of worm is involved.

Rising A term used in giving the age of a horse. A horse who is nearly six years old is said to be 'rising six'.

Roan A coat colouring consisting of an admixture of white hair with the body colour. If the body colour is black or black-brown, the admixture of white produces blue roan; if the body colour is bay or bay-brown, the admixture of white produces bay or red roan; if the body colour is chestnut, the admixture of white produces strawberry roan.

Roaring An abnormal noise made by the horse when breathing in.

Rolled-toe shoe A type of shoe designed to prevent stumbling.

Roller A leather, jute or webbing strap which goes around the body and is used to keep a sheet or rug in place.

Roller-pad Thick padding which sits oneither side of the horse's spine and prevents the roller from pressing on the backbone.

Roughage Bulk foods such as grass and hay. *Also known as* bulk food.

Rowel A wheel inserted at the head of a spur.

Run-out The action of a horse who ducks to the side of or round an obstacle instead of jumping it.

Running martingale A martingale consisting of a broad strap, one end of which is fitted to the girth. The strap passes between the forelegs, through the loop of a supporting neck strap, and divides into two branches. Each branch ends with a metal ring through which the reins are passed. It is designed to prevent undue raising of the head by exerting pressure on the reins.

S

Saddle gall An injury caused by a badly fitting or dirty saddle.

Saddle horn A leather-covered metal projection at the front of a Western saddle, used for twisting the line around when roping cattle.

Saddle horse A wooden trestle-like stand used when cleaning or storing saddles.

Saddle mark Hair in the shape of a saddle left on when clipping. Designed to protect the horse's back.

Saddle tree The frame on which a saddle is built.

Saliva A clear alkaline fluid discharge into the mouth which moistens food and aids digestion.

Salt-lick A block of salt fitted into a holder and attached to the stable wall or to a fence.

Sandcrack A crack in the wall of the hoof extending from the ground surface upwards or from the coronary band downwards.

Sarcoid A tumour on the skin, which resembles a wart at first but grows rapidly and may ulcerate.

Sarcoma A tumour of closely packed cells, often highly malignant.

Sausage-boot A stuffed leather ring which is strapped around the pastern to prevent the heel of the shoe damaging the elbow when the horse is lying down.

Scapula *See* Shoulder-blade.

Sclera The white of the eye.

Scour Another name for diarrhoea.

Second thigh *See* Gaskin.

Seedy toe A separation of the wall and sole at the toe by a soft cheese-like material.

Sensitive lamina A membrane lining the pedal bone of the foot and interlocking with the insensitive lamina. Together these structures bind the hoof to the bone. The sensitive lamina contains blood vessels, the insensitive lamina does not.

Sepsis Infection of blood or tissues.

Septicaemia The presence of bacteria in blood.

Sesamoid bones Small bones inserted into the tendons where pressure occurs.

Sesamoiditis Inflammation of the sesamoid bones.

Set fair To put down a horse's bed.

Setfast *See* Azoturia.

Shavings Wood shavings used for bedding.

Shetland A breed of British native pony originating in the islands to the north of Scotland. *Also known as* a Sheltie.

Shin The front of the cannon bone.

Shivering An involuntary quivering of the muscles of the hind legs and tail and occasionally the forelegs. Cause unknown, probably the result of nerve damage.

Shoulder-blade The flat bone on the side of the chest to which the muscles of the shoulder and forearm are attached.

Shoulder-in A training exercise consisting of a lateral movement in which the horse is bent slightly from head to tail around the rider's inside leg.

Sidebone A false bone caused by hardening of the cartilages of the pedal bone.

Silage A bulk food made from young grass, cut but not dried, and either put into a clamp with the air excluded or sealed in large, airtight bags.

Sinus A body space containing blood or air.

Sinusitis Infected air sinuses of the head.

Sire The male parent of a horse or pony.

Skewbald A coat-colouring featuring irregular patches of brown and white hair.

Skip A plastic or metal container used in stables for collecting droppings.

Skirt The lower and forward part of the saddle which covers the metal spring bar.

Slab fracture A break in the third carpal bone in the knee joint, or third tarsal bone in the hock joint, in which bone is split so that a slab becomes detached in front of the joint.

Slip-head The headstrap and cheekpieces which support the bridoon in a double bridle.

Snaffle A bit consisting of a single jointed or unjointed mouthpiece.

Snip An isolated white mark in the region of the nostrils.

Sock A white leg mark extending from the coronet a short way up the leg.

Soft palate A membrane of muscle which separates the mouth from the pharynx (throat) except when the horse is swallowing.

Sole The undersurface of the foot, usually concave and non-weight-bearing.

Sound (1) Not lame. (2) Fit and healthy.

Spavin *See* Bog spavin and Bone spavin.

Speedicut An injury to the inside of the knee or hock caused by a knock from the inside of the toe of the opposite leg.

Splint An enlargement of the inside or outside of the splint bone.

Splint bone A slender bone on either side of the cannon bone.

Sprain Torn fibres in various parts of the body such as ligaments, muscles and tendons, caused by abnormal stretching, and resulting in bleeding and inflammation.

Spread fence An obstacle designed to test a horse's ability to jump width as well as height.

Spring-tree A saddle tree with a strip of flexible steel let into the tree on each side at the waist.

Stable rubber A cloth used during grooming to remove surface dust from the coat.

Stadium jumping Show jumping (US term).

Staircase fence A spread fence that is low on the take-off side and gradually rises in height, for example a triple bar.

Stale In horses, to urinate.

Standing martingale A martingale consisting of a broad strap which runs from the girth, between the forelegs, through the loop of a supporting neck strap and is fitted to the underside of a cavesson noseband or to the cavesson part of a flash noseband. It is designed to prevent undue raising of the head by exerting pressure on the nose.

Star A white mark on the forehead.

Stargazer A horse who holds his head very high.

Sternum The breast bone.

Stifle The joint in the upper hind leg that corresponds to the human knee. Formed by the lower end of the femur and the upper end of the tibia with a patella (kneecap) attached to the front.

Stirrup-bar A metal bar attached to the saddle tree to which the stirrup leather is attached.

Stocking A white leg-mark extending from the knee or hock to the coronet.

Strangles An infectious disease which is characterized by swellings in the throat.

Strapping The full grooming of a horse.

Straw The dried stalks of cereal plants after the grain has been removed.

Stress fracture A minute break in a bone, particularly the cannon.

Stringhalt An involuntary snatching up of a

hind leg and flexing of a hock when walking. Cause unknown, probably the result of injured nerves.

Stripe A narrow white mark down the face.

Strongyle *See* Redworm.

Strongyloides *See* Threadworm.

Stud (1) A horse-breeding establishment. (2) A small piece of metal which screws into a horse's shoe to provide grip.

Stud book A record book containing details of the pedigree stock of a particular breed of horse or pony.

Sugar beet A palatable, energy-producing foodstuff, usually purchased in cube form. It must be soaked before feeding.

Sulphanilamide Colourless, odourless white powder used to treat pneumonia, septicaemia and local infections.

Surcingle A webbing band fitted around the horse and positioned over the girth and across the top of the saddle.

Surgical shoe A specially shaped shoe designed to alleviate the effects of disease, injury or defective conformation.

Suspensory ligament A broad, elastic band of fibrous tissue behind, and attached to, the cannon bone.

Sweat scraper A half-moon-shaped tool fitted with a handle. It is used for removing excess sweat or water from a horse's coat.

Sweet itch A skin condition causing severe itchiness, the result of an allergic reaction to fly bites.

Synovial fluid A transparent, sticky fluid present in the joints and structures such as tendon sheaths, which it helps to lubricate.

T

Tail The end of the spinal column from the back of the croup.

Tail-guard A protective covering fitted over the horse's tail when travelling.

Tapeworm An internal parasite which can cause digestive upsets.

Tarsal bones Small bones in the hock joint.

Tarsus (1) The hock or spavin area. (2) The framework of the eyelid.

Tartar A build-up of scaly deposit on the teeth.

Tendon A fibrous cord which attaches muscle to bone.

Tendon-boots Boots designed to give protection to the tendons at the back of the leg.

Tetanus A disease caused by a bacterium (*clostridium tetani*) which lives in the soil and in body tissues. Symptoms include stiffness, rigid limbs and neck and difficulty in moving the jaws and swallowing.

Thigh Part of the hind leg, between the hip and the stifle.

Thorax The part of the body between the withers and shoulders and the diaphragm.

Thoroughpin Inflammation of the tendon sheath which encloses the deep digital flexor tendon as it passes behind the hock.

Threadworm A very small worm found in the intestines of foals.

Three-day event A competitive event comprising dressage, cross-country and show jumping, run in that order on separate days.

Throatlash A narrow strap, part of the headpiece of a bridle, which passes under the throat and fastens with a buckle.

Thrush A condition of the frog causing black, evil-smelling erosion which in a severe case might reach the sensitive laminae. Symptoms include lameness and contracted heels.

Tibia The long bone between the stifle joint and the hock joint which forms the gaskin or second thigh.

Tick An insect that lives on the skin and sucks blood.

Tips Shortened shoes used to protect the toes of a horse at grass. *Also known as* grass tips.

Toad eye The distinctive prominent eye of the Exmoor pony.

Top line The line of the horse's back from the neck to the end of the croup.

Trace clip A method of clipping a horse whereby the hair is removed from the underside of the neck and belly, between the forelegs, and from the upper part of the hind legs. Depending on the amount of hair removed, the clip may be low, medium or high.

Trace elements Very small amounts of minerals which are essential to the horse's diet. They include copper, iron and selenium.

Transition A change from one pace to another.

Trauma A wound, injury or severe shock.

Travelling-boots Boots which cover the legs from above or below the knee and hock down to the coronet. Used to protect the legs during travelling.

Treads Wounds to the coronet region caused by the horse treading on himself or being trodden on, usually while travelling.

Trimming Tidying up a horse by removing unwanted hairs under the jaws, down the legs and at the back of the fetlock, and pulling the mane and tail.

Trot A two-time pace in which the horse's legs move in alternate diagonal pairs with a moment of suspension. *See also* Collected trot, Extended trot, Medium trot, Working trot.

Trotting poles Heavy poles placed on or raised slightly above the ground and used for schooling purposes.

Tubbing Placing a horse's foot in a bucket of warm water.

Turn on the forehand A movement in which the horse's hind quarters move around the forelegs, which move in a small circle.

Twitch A length of cord looped through the top of a rod and applied to the horse's nose as a means of restraint.

Tying up *See* Azoturia.

U

Ultrasound therapy
The use of ultra high frequency sound waves (beyond the upper limit of human hearing) to reduce swelling and inflammation in muscles and tendons.

Undershot mouth A deformity in which the lower jaw protrudes beyond the upper jaw.

Upright fence In show jumping an obstacle such as a gate, set of rails or wall with one vertical plane.

Urticaria *See* Nettle rash.

V

Vaccination The injection of a vaccine to stimulate immunity to a disease.

Vaccine A solution containing live, altered or killed micro-organisms which stimulate immunity to a particular microbe when injected or administered by mouth.

Vein Part of the blood circulatory system consisting of a thin-walled tube containing valves which help to prevent back-flow.

Vertebra One of the 51 to 57 bones of the spinal column. There are 7 neck (cervical) vertebrae; 18 withers region (thoracic); 6 back (lumbar); 5 croup (sacral) and 15-21 tail (coccygeal).

Vice An act of atypical, usually unpleasant, behaviour such as biting or kicking, or a chronic habit such as crib-biting or weaving.

Vitamins Organic substances necessary in small quantities for normal growth and well-being.

Volte A circle of 6m (20ft) diameter.

W

Walk A four-time pace. *See also* Collected walk, Extended walk, Medium walk.

Wall The outer, protective layer of the foot, formed from horn.

Wall-eye An eye in which the iris lacks pigment, and which shows more white than usual around the pupil.

Warble flies Large flies which lay their eggs on a horse's coat. Once hatched, the larvae turn into maggots which burrow into the skin and migrate through the body.

Wart A fleshy or scaly growth on the skin.

Water brush A grooming brush with longer bristles than a body brush. For use on the mane, tail and feet.

Weaving A habit seen predominantly in stabled horses in which the horse repeatedly shifts his weight from one forelimb to the other, swinging his neck from side to side.

Welsh A breed of British native pony originating in Wales. There are four divisions within the breed: Welsh Mountain Pony (Section A of the Welsh Pony and Cob Society Stud Book); Welsh Pony (Section B); Welsh Cob (Section C); Welsh Cob (Section D).

Weymouth A bit used

N O P Q R S T U V W X Y Z

in conjunction with a snaffle to form a double bridle and usually consisting of a straight mouthpiece with a central port.

Whinny A horse's call of pleasure and expectation.

Whisperer A person who tames difficult horses.

Whistling A high-pitched noise made when the horse breathes in.

White face A marking in which the horse's forehead and the front of the face are white.

White line The junction of the wall of the foot with the sole.

Whiteworm (ascarid) A large, round, grey-coloured worm which may grow up to 30 cm (1ft) long and which can cause gut damage.

Whorl A circle or irregular arrangement of coat hairs.

Wind The horse's breathing: an important aspect of a soundness examination.

Windgall A soft swelling of a joint or tendon sheath. *Also known as* a wind puff.

Wind-sucking A habit in which the horse arches his neck and gulps in air but does not swallow it.

Wisp A pad of plaited straw used when grooming a stabled horse to help develop and harden muscle.

Withers The top of the shoulders, between the neck and back, formed by the 3rd to 9th thoracic vertebrae.

Wobbler syndrome A condition of poor coordination, especially of the hind legs, caused by damage to the spinal cord due to a developmental abnormality, or to trauma.

Working canter The pace between collected and medium canter.

Working trot The pace between collected and medium trot.

Worms *See* Lungworms, Pinworms, Redworms, Tapeworms, Whiteworms.

Wormer A drug designed to control worms in the horse's body.

X

X-ray Energy wave of the same type as light ray, but of much shorter wave-length. Used by veterinary surgeons when diagnosing various injuries/conditions.

Y

Yard (1)An open space adjoining and used in conjunction with stables. (2) The business or premises of people who keep horses.

Yawing The action of a ridden horse which fights with its head, reaching downwards and outwards.

Yew The most poisonous tree native to Britain. If eaten by a horse it depresses the action of the heart, usually causing instant death.

Youngstock A term used to describe horses up to and including the age of three or four.

N
O
P
Q
R
S
T
U
V
W
X
Y
Z

Z

Zebra An equine animal native to Africa. There are three types of zebra: plains or Burchell's, mountain, and Grevy's, which is the largest and most horse-like.

Zebra marks Stripes on the limbs, neck and withers or quarters of a horse. Believed to be primitive features.

Zonkey The offspring of a zebra and a donkey.

Abbreviations

AHS   Arab Horse Society.

AHSA   American Horse Shows Association.

BDS   British Driving Society. Founded in 1957 to encourage and assist anyone interested in the driving of equine animals.

BEF   British Equestrian Federation. The national governing body for horse sports in the United Kingdom. The BEF is affiliated to the FEI (Fédération Équestre Internationale).

BEVA   British Equine Veterinary Association.

BFSS   British Field Sports Society.

BHS   British Horse Society.

BHSAI   British Horse Society Assistant Instructor.

BHSII   British Horse Society Intermediate Instructor.

BHSI   British Horse Society Instructor.

BSJA   British Showjumping Association. The governing body of the sport of show jumping in Great Britain.

BSPS   British Show Pony Society.

BVMS/BVM&S Bachelor of Veterinary Medicine and Surgery.

BVSc   Bachelor of Veterinary Science.

CDI   Concours de Dressage Internationale (international dressage show).

CDIO   Concours de Dressage Internationale Officiel (official international dressage show, i.e. one that includes a team competition).

CDI-W   An international dressage show staging a Dressage World Cup qualifier.

CIC   Concours Internationale Complet (international horse trials).

CCI   Concours Complet Internationale (international three-day event).

CCIO   Concours Complet Internationale Officiel (official international three-day event, i.e. one that includes a team competition).

CHIO   Concours Hippique Internationale Officiel (official international horse show staging more than one discipline and including team competitions).

COPD   Chronic Obstructive Pulmonary Disease. A chronic respiratory condition caused by sensitivity to dust in the atmosphere and the mould in hay and straw, and a common cause of chronic coughing.

CSI   Concours de Saut Internationale (international jumping show).

CSIO   Concours de Saut International Officiel (official international jumping show, i.e. one staging a Nations Cup).

CSI-W   An international jumping show staging a Show Jumping World Cup qualifier.

DBS   Donkey Breed Society.

EHPS   Endurance Horse and Pony Society of Great Britain. The governing body of endurance riding in Britain.

FBHS   Fellow of the British Horse Society.

FEI   Fédération Équestre Internationale (International Equestrian Federation). The international governing body of the equestrian sports of dressage, driving, endurance riding, eventing, reining, show jumping and vaulting.

FRCVS   Fellow of the Royal College of Veterinary Surgeons.

G   Gelding.

GSB   General Stud Book. The stud book of the Thoroughbred horse, founded in 1791 and containing all Thoroughbred mares and their progeny foaled in the British Isles.

hh   Hands high.

HOYS   Horse of the Year Show.

M&M   Mountain and Moorland (mountain and moorland ponies of the British Isles).

MFH   Master of Foxhounds.

MRCVS   Member of the Royal College of Veterinary Surgeons.

NPS   National Pony Society.

NSAID   Nonsteroidal anti-inflammatory drug (for example phenylbutazone or 'bute').

RDA   Riding for the Disabled.

RIHS   Royal International Horse Show.

RVCS   Royal College of Veterinary Surgeons.

TB   Thoroughbred.

UKCC   United Kingdom Coaching Certificate.

USDF   United States Dressage Federation.

USEA   United States Eventing Association.

USEF   United States Equestrian Federation. The national governing body for most equestrian sports in the USA.

WHP   Working hunter pony.

Test your knowledge of the equestrian world with
The Pony Club Quiz Book 2

Another 1001 questions with 4 levels of difficulty.
Compiled by Judith Draper

ISBN 978-1-907279-09-6

The 1001 questions in *The Pony Club Quiz Book 2* will test your knowledge of all aspects of equestrianism. Perfect for Pony Club members and non-members alike, there is a challenge for everyone—novice or expert, young and old—and however deep their involvement in the horse and pony world.

Subjects range from general horsemastership to the horse in history, war, folklore, literature, music and art. The whole spectrum of equestrian sport is represented: from mounted games and tetrathlon to racing, and from show jumping and polo to reining and carriage driving.

This is an absorbing, informative and entertaining book which you will keep dipping into again and again.

The Pony Club Equine Dictionary has been compiled by equestrian writer Judith Draper, who for many years covered major horse shows and events for national newspapers and international magazines. She is the author of a number of books, including *The Book of the Horse* and the successful children's series *My First Pony*, *My First Pony Care*, and *My First Pony Show*.

Also published by The Pony Club:

The Manual of Horsemanship
The Instructor's Handbook
Building Show Jumping Courses
Keeping a Pony at Grass
Junior Road Rider
To Be a Dressage Rider
A Young Person's Guide to Eventing
Pasture Management
Stablemates: Vital Statistics—A Guide to Conformation
Quiz Books 1, 2 and 3
Sticker Books 1, 2 and 3
The Pony Club Activity Book
'Look...No Hands!'—Straightforward Cross-Country

Visit www.pcuk.org for a full and up-to-date list of Pony Club publications and to find out more information.